The Surprised Sprite

by Kay Brophy

with illustrations by Katy Boys

First published in the UK in 2017 by Middle Farm Press
British Library Cataloguing-in-Publication Data
A catalogue record for this book is available from the British Library
ISBN 978-0-9928896-8-5
This edition 2019
2 3 4 5 6 7 8 9 10

Published by Middle Farm Press
Author: Kay Brophy
Managing Editor: Kate Taylor
Illustrator: Katy Boys
Designer: Su Richards
Printed by Think Digital Books Ltd

Acorn
MIDDLE FARM PRESS

To my sister, Charlotte

Lifeland
Station
STATION OF SURPRISE
ANGER ARCHES
SAD STONES

FOREST OF FEAR
DISGUSTING DUMP
HAPPINESS HILLS
DUMP
DISGUSTING
DUMP
FOREST OF FEAR
HAPPINESS HILLS

There once lived a Sprite,
clever but lazy
She was such a show-off,
she drove people crazy
She lived in Lifeland,
in the old town
Noisy and loud, bossing
people around

SHOE
CURLY'S SALON

The Sprite was rude
and terrible at sharing
Words fell out of her mouth;
she spoke without caring

She didn't understand rules
or what they were for
She found being nice
a bit of a chore

'I don't have to be kind, people do as I say!'
'If they choose not to listen, I shoo them away!'
'I am queen of Lifeland, and all things are good'
'The people here need me so
they do as they should'

So the Sprite was happy being this way
She was in charge,
but one hot summer's day

Someone nearby was getting fed up
He was about to explode;
he had just had enough

'Go get my shoes, fetch my hat, tidy up'

'And when you've finished, go get that cup'

'I don't like this blanket, move it away'

'Come on, hurry up,

just do as I say'

Sprite's only friend was
a young boy called Dan
He was angry with Sprite and
he needed a plan

He'd had quite enough of being treated like this
It was not a good friendship, something was amiss

But Dan was frightened of
what Sprite could do
People called her a bully;
was that really true?
Sprite had been mean so often before
But he'd had enough, he couldn't
take any more

I Love MY best Friend *SPRITE*
MY
Lis
1.
From the bakery for Sprite
2. Make
Ham
picnic
3. S
4.

Dan opened his mouth and his words
were quite clear
'I have something to say,
something you need to hear!'
'I am angry and unhappy being bossed around'
'So I am leaving' he said
with a serious frown

'Are you joking? But why?

We are friends, we have fun'

'I am shocked and surprised...

what have I done?'

'I don't need you anyway,
in fact I'm going too'
And with a flick of her hair,
off the Sprite flew

STATION OF SURPRISE

She ran away from the town,
as far as she could
Not stopping to rest or think if she should
She arrived at a station, with a train
waiting there
Where was it going?
She didn't care

So she boarded the train and her journey began
She had plenty of time now, to think of HER plan
Lost in 'big' feelings, confused and alone
Quietly thinking about her
friends and her home

FRAGILE
1
2
3

Sprite's journey was long

and full of surprise

She learnt many things; Lostland opened her eyes

So a different Sprite, after much contemplation

Headed back down the path,

away from the station

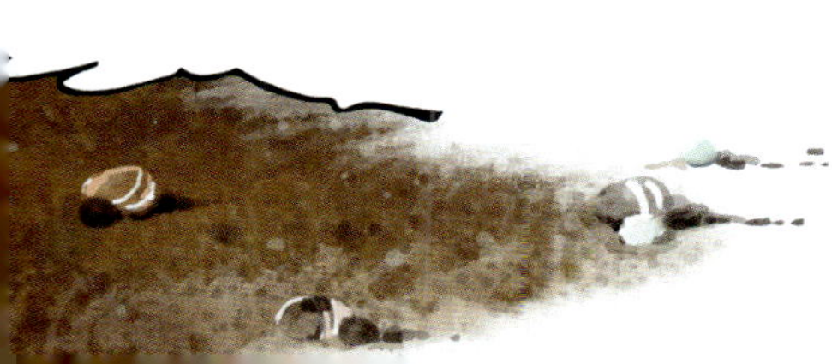

She returned to a party and people she knew
She was invited to join them so over she flew
The Sprite discovered something
important that day
Surprises can happen in all kinds of ways

USER GUIDE FOR TEACHERS, PARENTS AND CARERS

All children, in every walk of life, will struggle with their feelings from time to time. The Surprised Sprite is part of a series of books called Finding Your Way. Each book takes one of the six 'big' feelings of sadness, fear, anger, happiness, surprise and disgust and aims to show the reader how to explore, identify and manage the feeling safely on their own or with the help of an adult.

HOW TO USE THIS BOOK

This book can be read with a child or a group of children at any time. It will be particularly useful if the child is, or has been, surprised. Rather than focusing on the child themselves, the adult should focus on the characters' feelings. For example, talking about how the Sprite is feeling will help the child to feel safe to talk. Adults can use the pictures within the book to aid them.

USING THE FIVE Ws

Example questions you could ask while reading this book:

- **W**hy does the Sprite need help?
- **W**hat do you think she should do?
- **W**here is she in Lifeland?
- **W**ho helps her to deal with her feelings?
- **W**hen does the Sprite feel happy?

Sometimes children can experience feelings such as surprise, sadness, anger and fear all at once. Adults can help the child explore these feelings using the 'Lifeland' map at the front of the book. As you read through the book together try to encourage the child to think about where the Sprite is on the map. For example, when the Sprite is on the train you could help them think about where that might be on the map, exploring feelings and places together.

DID YOU KNOW?

- Reading with your child at least four times a week can help them to develop their own reading and literacy skills.
- Talking to your child about feelings can help them develop their emotional language and intelligence.

Kay's Surprise PARTY
Dragon lemonade
Kay